Camping

Beginners basics!

A guide to equipment and tips for happy camping!

(im)PulsePaperbacks

Let's go camping!

Many people are re-discovering camping. It's a great, affordable way to get away from the hustle and bustle of day-to-day life for a couple of days, weeks or even months! A camping trip can be a spur of the moment decision or a holiday planned well in advance – either way if you choose the right location, go with your family, or a group of friends, or just the dog, you are guaranteed to have a great time.

Camping is a simple pleasure that you can do all year round, depending on where you choose to go, and allows you the flexibility to move from place to place if the desire takes you. For some, the thought of camping brings childhood memories flooding back, and camping is a great way to spend quality time with loved ones, to kick-back, relax and soothe the soul!

Planning your trip

Deciding where to go is the first step. If you have friends or family members who regularly camp, ask their advice about good sites - there is nothing quite like a personal recommendation from someone you trust. Another good source of information is obviously the internet. There are a number of specific sites geared towards finding a suitable campsite, many of which are searchable by country, region or town and also include independent traveller reviews which may also help you choose. For camping in the UK and Europe one of the better websites is **www.campingandcaravanningclub.co.uk** which is easily navigable. For camping in Australia a good website is **www.camping.com.au** and try **www.nzcamping.co.nz** for information on campsites in New Zealand.

When planning your trip you can choose from a variety of locations depnding on whether you are looking for peace and tranquillity or action packed days.

Most sites offer amenities such as fresh water, toilets, and showers and some even have electricity hook-ups. However, some are more remote and rustic and do not provide such facilities. Check the campsite advertisement or website for the facilities provided. If you are unsure of anything call ahead.

A number of sites offer nearby attractions such as, cycle routes, hiking trails and lakes for fishing. Others offer special activities like kayaking and rock climbing. You will find many designed to attract families that have swimming pools and fun activities like mini-golf.

Pick a site and area that offers the kind of setting and activities that will suit you and your party.

Another factor to consider is the distance. You don't want the tiredness that results from long drives to cancel out the rejuvenation camping affords - and don't forget you still have to erect the tent when you get there!

For a weekend getaway, driving for no more than 3 hours away from home is advisable.

If you are having trouble picking a site, visit a local camping and outdoor shop. Usually the employees there are outdoor enthusiasts and will be able to give you some advice.

Book your campsite before leaving. Even if you have been advised that booking is not essential, it is recommended to ensure you will get a pitch. It is especially important to book over Bank Holidays and during School Holidays as some sites will be fully booked many months in advance.

Choosing your tent

There are many factors to consider when choosing a tent.

Size

Make sure your tent has one berth for each person sleeping in it. Don't overcrowd your tent. You will use any extra space for the storage of all of your equipment.

Weather conditions

If you intend to camp throughout the year it is advisable to make sure the tent is fully waterproof and it is a good idea to have a tent with a porch to store your outdoor gear. If you will be camping mostly in the sun and hotter climates, consider lighter coloured tents as darker colours absorb the heat and the tent can get very hot inside.

Ease of use

Sizes and styles of tents vary, as does their ease of putting up. If you are considering mostly short breaks, you do not want to spend 2 hours or more each trip erecting and dismantling your tent.

Types of Tents

Here is a brief guide to the types of tents on the market. This will give you an idea of what type of tent may suit your needs, but we recommend visiting camping shops especially the larger ones that host camping exhibitions. These are usually held at Garden Centres and all the models of tents are erected so you can go inside and try them out for size.

Dome Tents

These tents are usually quite simple to erect. They consist of 2 or 3 poles that pass through the centre of the roof to form the main part of the tent. They can also have separate bedroom pods, up to as many as 4. They come in many sizes, including some hybrid dome/tunnels. Some models also have porches that are ideal for outdoor storage. Ideally choose a tent which has a sewn-in ground sheet, which will stop any unwanted visitors from entering your tent such as bugs and spiders.

For: Good headroom - some models allow you to stand up inside easily.
Against: These tents can be unstable in high winds.

Vis-a-vis

This is a term that applies to tents with sleeping compartments on either side of a living area. The basic tent can be either ridge or dome style. Most are made of lightweight nylon or polyester.

For: Easy to put up.
Against: Separate ground sheet for the living area – not a good idea if you don't want creepy crawlies.

Pyramid Tent

This is the original basic tent with a tarpaulin hung over a central pole and pegged to the ground. Very easy to erect.

For: Very easy to set up.
Against: Separate ground sheet. Not great headroom.

Tunnel Tent

This tent is shaped like a tunnel which is higher at the front (where the door usually is) and tapers down to the rear. You can just about sit up in the front of these tents. They have a single or dual pole design with the longer pole at the front. The strength and durability can vary greatly depending on size, type and poles.

For: A very lightweight tent.
Against: Can be cramped inside.

Cabin Tents

These tents are great for families and groups and are usually used for car camping, as they are heavy. They have separate bedroom compartments and allow you to stand up straight in the living area. It is important that these tents are erected correctly making sure the fabric does not sag and collect water.

For: **Lots of space.**
Against: **Heavy. Fairly difficult to set up.**

Geodesic tents

These are very similar to the dome tents, except that they have a different pole configuration. The flexible poles cross at different levels and hold the fabric taut. They are better suited than most other tents for windy conditions as they do not need much anchoring, they are also easier to pitch on rocky or uneven ground.

For: **Easy to position and site.**
Against: **Heavier than tunnels, longer to erect.**

Extras

Gazebos

These are not strictly tents and are not intended to sleep in. They are great if you are sleeping in a smaller sized tent and provide a living area. They are also good for providing shade on a hot day, and shelter if it is wet, but they can be unstable in high winds.

Windbreaks

These do what they say on the tin and keep the wind down if you are trying to eat a meal and are great for providing a level of privacy.

Picnic Mat

It is a good idea to include a picnic mat, these are available with plastic backing which keeps them dry if the ground is damp and can be used outside the tent to create additional lounging or sitting space.

Before you go...

Make sure you have all the parts of the tent and they are all in working order.

If you are a newbie or have just bought a new tent, set it up in your back garden or wherever you can.

Get used to doing it, take it down then put it up again so you can literally do it in your sleep.

Also practice packing it away - this can be taxing and there is often a 'knack' to how the tent fits in the bag.

GEAR LIST

- TENT
- SLEEPING BAG
- THERMA-REST
- POT SET
- WHISPERLITE STOVE
- FUEL BOTTLE
- FUEL
- SHOVEL
- BACKPACK
- DOWN JACKET
- SHELL
- FLEECE
- GORE TEX PANTS
- FLEECE PANT
- LONG JOHNS

- LANTERN
- HEAD LAMP
- SNOW SHOES
- POLES
- GAITERS
- ZIP LOCKS
- THERMOS
- SPOON TOOL
- MULTI TOOL
- MUG
- PLATE

- T.P.
- WATER BOTTLES

TO GET
☒ FOOD ☒
- GORP
- OAT MEAL
- BAGELS
- GARBAGE BAGS

Equipment

Within reason, keep most of your camping equipment in one big storage tub or designated area. When organising a camping trip you do not want to spend hours having to rummage through the attic/shed/garage and make last minute runs to the shop to gather all the supplies you'll need.

To avoid this, simply keep most of your camping equipment together. Once you have your camping box loaded up, whenever the urge to tear out into the country strikes, you can just grab it and go. Keep the following supplies in the box. Specific supplies may vary according to what kind of activities you'll be doing, where you're going, and what season it is. But this covers the basics:

Tent
Sleeping bags
Sleeping pads/air-mattress
First aid kit
Lantern
Flashlight
Extra batteries
Wet wipes/bacterial hand wash
Matches
Insect repellent
Bin bags
Ziplock bags
Stove/Fuel
Plates/Cups/Cutlery
Water bottle
All purpose tool/Swiss Army Knife
Toilet Roll

Create a permanent checklist that you can consult prior to each trip. This will consist of the items that won't fit in a tub or need to be packed right before leaving, such as perishables. Include on the list:

Sunscreen
Camp or lawn chairs
Clothes (Everyday and anything required for chosen activities such as hiking)
Food
Food Storage (coolers etc)
Toiletries

Daytime Clothing

You need to pack for the climate and the type of holiday you are planning. If it is likely to rain, it is advisable to invest in some waterproofs and wellies for everyone; this will save your clothes from getting wet. Remember to pack light as space will be limited, and many campsites have washing and drying facilities.

Sleeping gear

Your sleeping gear is very important and it can make or break a camping trip. If you don't sleep well it can ruin the whole mood of your trip and won't make for happy campers. Dress for bed depending on the weather. In the summer months it generally still gets quite chilly at night so warm clothing is still advisable. In the colder months really dress for bed in fleece pyjamas and socks as the temperature can really dip at night. To keep warmer, wear a hat to sleep in, as 80% of heat loss occurs through your head.

Sleep tight

Sleeping bags

The standard rectangle shape sleeping bag and the mummy shaped ones are the most common. The mummy bags are better if you will be camping in colder conditions, with some being suitable for conditions of up to -10c, which is seriously cold weather. Another new style on the market is the Selk Bag™. This has arms and legs; it is a sleeping bag you can wear! You can unzip the ends of the arms so you can still use your hands. At the end of your camping trip it can take several attempts trying to get your sleeping bag back in its carry case all neatly rolled up. If you are struggling you can simply get the sleeping bag back into its carry bag by stuffing it. It will fit, it's quick, and it won't harm the sleeping bag. Try it sometime!

Finally, don't forget your pillow. Most people like to take the pillow off their own bed for a bit of 'home comfort'.

Tip

Air sleeping bags once a day. Even the best sleeping bags trap your sweat at night and need a good airing.

Bedtime

There are a selection of beds you can use for camping.

Air Mattresses

These are easy to use. You can inflate them by simply using a pump that you plug into your car cigarette lighter, which only takes a few minutes. They are very comfortable. You may find after a couple of nights you need to give them a top up of air to keep them firm.

These are also not very good if you are on a slope, you keep rolling off!! One other thing to note is that if you put a blanket or throw underneath your sleeping bag it can stop you from getting cold in the winter and sweaty in the summer.

Camp beds

These can be a little tricky to put together in the beginning but once you get the hang of them you can put them up in no time.

You can put a blanket underneath your sleeping bag and a big throw over the top of you and you should have a wonderful nights sleep.

Mats

If you really want to go basic then you can just use a mat. It all depends on how much gear you want to take and if you think you can manage sleeping on the floor.

Camping mats are not expensive and they good if you are hiking and camping where you need to carry your kit with you.

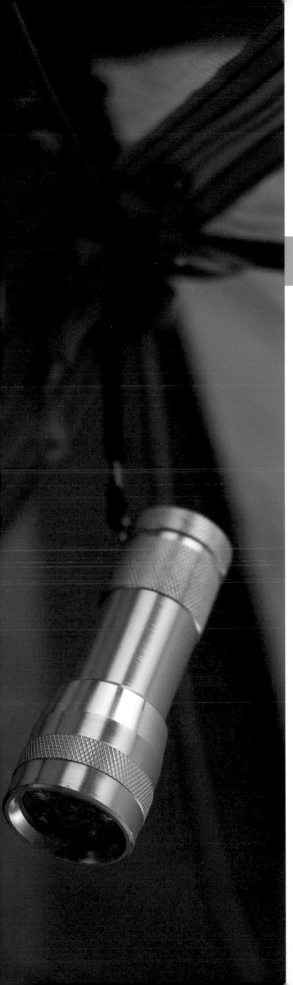

Lighting

You will need several different types of lights, lamps and torches. They can either be gas, battery powered (regular or rechargeable), solar or hand-cranked. The gas lamps are really good for use outside the tent; they give good light and one canister of gas lasts quite a while. NEVER use the gas lamps inside the tent as they are a fire risk.

Use battery powered lamps for inside the tent. The best are the rechargeable ones that you charge either by mains or car; make sure you fully charge them before you leave for your trip. If you are using regular battery powered lighting remember to pack extra batteries.

It is always good to have a few small hand-torches inside the tent for that emergency dash to the loo, or when you are desperately trying to find your pj's without waking everyone else up!

Head torches (shown above) are very practical as you have both hands free but you just have to get over looking a bit 'All the gear - no idea'.

You can pick these up at any camping store. They are great for cooking in the dark!

Camping stoves

There are many variations of portable stoves. Firstly there is your basic one-ring burner. This attaches directly to a gas canister and is simple to use. For more heavy duty cooking there is the two-ring stove/grill but you will need quite a large gas bottle for these. One of the best is the portable one-ring stove in a case. These are powered by an aerosol bottle of gas that is fitted inside the case which is very handy. They are very portable and excellent for taking on picnics and days out. Alternatively, many people like to cook on BBQ's when they are camping. Disposable BBQ's are readily available from all good supermarkets or camping stores.

Camp Kitchen

You can buy a camping kitchen from any good camping store. It is a matter of personal choice and space as to whether you need one or not. They are similar to a portable kitchen cabinet that will hold your stove and provide a food preparation area. They usually have a cupboard underneath which allows storage of your cooking equipment and non-perishable food. They are packed flat and can sometimes take a while to put up. If you are going on a longer holiday and intend to do plenty of cooking this may come in handy. Plastic storage tubs with lids are a great alternative to store all of your kitchen equipment on and off the campsite.

Tables and chairs

It is a matter of personal choice for tables and chairs. You can buy the integrated picnic table and 4 seats which folds up into a handy size or choose to have separate camping chairs that you can move around your campsite. The fold-up variety is a good choice and are generally inexpensive. When choosing a table you should try to go for the most sturdy, as remember you won't necessarily be on hard ground.

Coolers

It is very important that you keep your perishable food cold. Cooler bags are inexpensive and do the job. They are available from most supermarkets. A good choice is a cooler box. They keep the food colder for longer as they have more insulation. You can also use blue ice and it is a good idea to take an extra set as most campsites have facilities for you to freeze them. Taking frozen food is also a good idea as you can keep it in the cooler and it keeps the other food cold. A more expensive alternative is the electric cooler. These are good if you are not camping for too long or if you have got an electric hook up. They also work off the car cigarette lighter. One down side is the size of the cooler, the actual space inside is not that large as they incorporate the motor. They are ideal for car journeys and days out. These are available from camping stores and motoring shops.

For the absolute best, go for a camping fridge. These work in exactly the same way as the fridge in your kitchen and are powered either by electricity or gas. Good camping stores will stock these. Another way you can keep food cool or, at least, at a constant temperature is submerging items in cold water and ice. Remember to keep changing the water and adding more ice.

Tips

To remove odours from your cooler, wipe with a water and baking soda solution.
Use a separate cooler for drinks so as not to open the food cooler too often.
Replenish your ice often. Keep your food cold at all times to avoid food spoilage and food poisoning.
All items in your cooler should be packed in watertight bags or containers.
Fill 2 litre drink/milk bottles with water or juice and freeze. They keep the cooler cold and provide a cold drink.
To fix a cooler leak, apply melted paraffin wax inside and outside the leaky area.

Pots and Pans

What pots and pans you need with you will depend on what you intend to cook. If you have any old pans that you don't use anymore these are a good addition to your camping kit so you will always have them available. The same can be said for plates and bowls and it is good to have some crockery, as it is nicer to eat from proper plates. Great picnic sets which have plates, bowls, cutlery, cups and plastic glasses are available from camping stores and generally include everything you will need to eat a meal. It is always a good idea to include paper plates and cups for snacks and drinks, as this will reduce the washing up! Remember to take cooking utensils.

Serving spoon
Fish slice
Tongs
Wooden spoon
Can opener
Corkscrew
Peeler
2 x sharp knives
Kitchen scissors
Chopping mats
Measuring jug
Mixing bowl
Tin Foil

When deciding what food to take with you it is a good idea to find out whether you will have local shops or supermarkets nearby. If you are in a remote location you will need to take all of your food with you.

Preparation

Whilst you are still in the comfort of your fully stocked and well equipped kitchen, you can make life easier for you on your trip by preparing food stuffs in advance. Chop and measure ingredients for each meal ahead of time and pack in ziplock bags. Label each bag accordingly so that you know which ingredients you need for each meal. You can prepare soups, stews, pasta sauces or chilli etc ahead of time. Put in ziplock bags, freeze and keep until your trip, where you can load them into your cooler. They can be reheated on site for a quick meal.

Storage

Ziplock bags in various sizes can be very useful for food storage. To avoid unwanted visits from animals, keep food stored away or hang above ground level. Take lots of plastic airtight boxes in a variety of sizes. They are great for storing anything from matches to sugar to washing powder. Disposable water bottles make great dispensers for salad dressings, oils and sauces - remember that you should decant as much as possible into smaller, more manageable bottles geared towards the length of your trip.

Cooking tips

To cook hamburgers more evenly throughout, put a hole in the middle of your hamburger about the size of your finger, during grilling the hole will disappear but the centre will be cooked the same as the edges. Pita bread is easier to pack and stays in better shape while camping than regular type breads.

When barbequing chicken, cook the chicken without the sauce until it is halfway cooked, then coat with sauce. The sauce won't burn onto the chicken and you can ensure the chicken is cooked thoroughly. Apply oil on your camp grill to keep foods from sticking, and make it easier to clean (unless of course you are using a disposable BBQ pack!). On your last day of camp, use your leftover meats and vegetables to make omelettes for breakfast. You can use almost any ingredient in omelettes. Then you don't have to take the leftovers home with you.

Fire-side hints

If you can, ensure that you use fireproof cooking equipment and keep handles away from extreme heat and flames. Cover pots whenever cooking outdoors which will ensure that the food will cook faster and you will save on fuel. This will also keep dirt and insects out of your food.

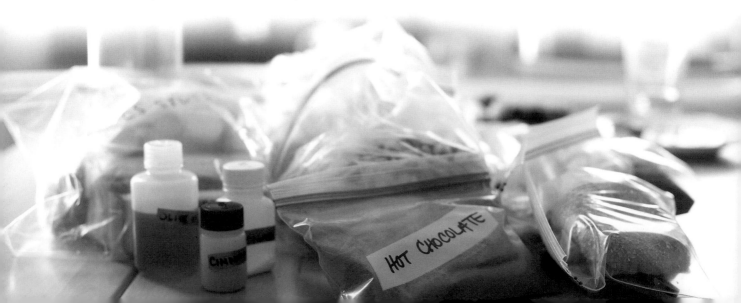

To easily remove burnt on food from your pot or pan, simply add a drop or two of washing-up liquid and enough water to cover the bottom of the pan and bring to a boil. You can also protect your pots and pans from smoke and fire damage, by applying a liquid soap on the outside of your pots and pans before putting over the fire.

If the campsite does not have facilities for you to wash your pots and dishes, put a pan of hot water on the fire while you eat so that it'll be ready for washing up when you are done. Obviously you should NOT place your hands in boiling water.

The food you take with you on your trip will be dependant upon many factors, not least of which is how long you are going for, the season you are travelling, how many will be going etc. Even if you think there is no need to go to the trouble of preparing food and taking it with you - you may be planning on eating out most of the time - there are still a few basics that it doesn't hurt to have with you.

Cooking oil	**Baked beans and tinned foods**	**Bacon and eggs**
Bread and butter	**Salt and Pepper**	**Spices and herbs**
Sugar	**Fruit**	**Vegetables**
Coffee and tea	**Milk and soft drinks**	**Pasta and rice**
Condiments	**Alcohol**	

Try these delicious easy to make recipes on your next camping trip.

Porridge with apples (Serves 2)

2 cups porridge oats (not instant)
3 cups water
1 large apple, peeled and sliced

1. Put the water in a large saucepan and boil. When boiling, pour in the porridge and stir for 1-2 minutes. At this point you should turn the heat down while stirring but if your stove does not simmer just lift the pot away from the heat for a few seconds periodically.

2. After a minute, put in the apple slices and continue to stir for a further 30-45 seconds. The porridge should be thickening up by this point. If not, keep it on the heat a little longer. Take the pot off the heat, cover the porridge and set aside for a couple of minutes.

Serve, with any extras such as brown sugar or some honey drizzled over. You could also replace up to half of the water with milk while you are cooking the porridge for a creamier version.

Campfire fry-up (Serves 4)

6 strips of bacon
1 small tin new potatoes or cooked potatoes
1 onion or red/green pepper
4 eggs

1. Place the 6 strips of bacon on a large piece of tin foil, leaving enough room to create a loose foil parcel. Chop the new potatoes into fairly small pieces and cover bacon with them. If you do not have tinned potatoes, use left-over potatoes from the night before.

2. Cut 4 rings of onion or bell peppers and place on top of potatoes. Crack an egg into each ring and season with salt and pepper. Wrap the foil securely and place into the fire. Cook for 10 to 15 minutes or until the eggs and bacon are done.

Campfire Chicken Parcels (Serves 4)

4 chicken breasts
1 can of pineapple slices
4 large squares of tin foil
1 small green pepper, chopped
1/2 of a small red pepper, chopped
Handful button mushrooms, chopped
1 teaspoon of butter or margarine

1. Divide the peppers and mushrooms into four equal portions. Coat a small area in the centre of each piece of tin foil with the butter or margarine.

2. Place one portion of the peppers and mushrooms onto the greased area of tin foil. Place the chicken breast on top and a pineapple slice on top of the chicken breast. Season with salt and pepper.

3. Fold tin foil over securely so there are no leaks. Repeat with the rest of the ingredients so you have four individual servings. Place onto hot grill or coals for approximately 15 minutes, then turnover and cook for another ten to fifteen minutes.

Sausage casserole (Serves 4)

8 sausages
1 tin chopped tomatoes
1 sliced onion
Handful of sliced mushrooms
1 beef stock cube
Tomato puree
Dash of red wine

1. Fry the sausage gently to brown all sides and partly cook through, then remove from pan and keep warm. Fry the onions and mushrooms in the pan until soft, then add the tinned tomatoes, the stock cube and puree mixed in half to 3/4 pint of boiling water and bring to the boil.

2. Reduce the heat, put the sausages back in the pan, add a good dash of red wine and cook until the sausages are cooked through.

3. Serve with mashed potatoes and peas.

Happy camping tips!

Don't take valuables or sentimental items camping, in case they get lost, broken or stolen.

Space blankets work great for unexpected cool weather. They are inexpensive and when folded up they fit in your back pocket.

Always bring a roll of duct tape. It can be used for lots of things!

Always take hats and gloves – even in the middle of summer it can get quite cold in the evening.

Always clear the rubbish away before you go to bed – preferably dispose of it in the bin store or keep in your car to prevent foxes and other unwanted visitors - although if you do this, dispose of it as soon as possible the next day.

To keep matches dry - dip the match stick in wax and when needed, scrape off the tip of the match and light. Also keep matches in a waterproof container.

To keep soap clean at your campsite, put it in a sock or a zip lock bag. You can also use antibacterial hand gel cleansers - these are great for cleaning your hands prior to and after cooking and eating.

Without spoiling your camping fun, be sensible and safe when camping to ensure that everybody has a great time. Here are a few essential tips to remember to keep you all happy campers!

Read and adhere to the rules of the campsite
Campsite rules are there to ensure that all visitors enjoy their holiday whilst keeping safe. Campsite rules will differ from site to site but are generally posted in an easily accessible area, so there is no excuse for not adhering to these.

Remember tents are flammable
Although many newer tents are treated to be flame retardant, tents can burn so be sure to set up any open fires well away from tents.

Fire precautions and evacuation points
Make sure you know the fire precaution arrangements on the site and be aware of any evacuation and assembly points. Do not place cooking, heating or lighting appliances near the sides or the roof of the tent and always carefully observe the safety instructions for these appliances. Never allow children to play near lighted appliances. Keep the exits of the tent clear so in the unlikely event of needing to evacuate this can be done quickly and safely.

Gas
Be very careful with gas canisters. Keep upright at all times. Keep outside in a well-ventilated area. Check for leakage by putting soap liquid on all connections. Always turn off when you are not using them.

Around the campfire
Pick a spot downwind so the breeze will blow the smoke away from your tent. Build your fire on a bed of sand or dirt away from logs or stumps and vegetation. Clear away any material that could catch fire. Be careful what you burn. Plastics can give off noxious fumes and aerosols and sealed containers can explode. Put your fire out each night by covering it with sand or dirt or dousing it with water.

Personal safety
Use campsites. It may be tempting to just pitch in the middle of nowhere and set up for a few days but it is essential that you let people know where you are for your own safety. DO NOT be tempted to set up camp on land without the owners consent, and if you are female campers travelling alone you may wish to invest in a personal safety device.

Weather wise
In very damp or cold weather ensure that your tent and equipment is suited to the conditions. If not, try again another day when the weather is better. Extreme or all weather camping really is for the seasoned camper.

Selecting a pitch

It goes without saying that wherever possible you should try and arrive at your destination with enough daylight left for you to select your pitch and erect your tent. When you arrive at the campsite have a look around before you decide where to pitch your tent.

Select an area that is as flat as possible but avoid marshy, low lying ground that could flood in a sudden downpour.

Look for an area that is away from the campsite entrance as you do not want to be disturbed at night by people returning from a night out. Try to get the right distance from the toilets, not too close as this will be a high traffic area, but close enough for a midnight dash!

Avoid pitching your tent under trees, especially in windy weather. Many give off a sticky sap that will be difficult to remove and also may compromise your waterproofing. Make use of any natural windbreaks, hedges, walls or boulders and, where possible, face the tent door away from the prevailing wind.

Remove all stones, sticks or anything that might damage the groundsheet from the area you have selected to erect your tent. For extra protection place a sheet of sturdy polythene beneath the groundsheets, especially under lightweight tents. This also keeps the groundsheet clean.

When siting your tent, ensure a minimum distance of 6m between adjacent tents or awnings to ensure safety and relative privacy for you and your neighbouring campers.

Pitching your tent

Pitch your tent with all the zips closed.

Drive the pegs in at an angle to the direction of pull to get the best grip in the ground.

Rubber guy loops should be stretched sufficiently to tension the fabric without over-stretching.

Pegs situated at the base of zips should be crossed over to take off any strain.

Keep zips clean, especially the spiral type, if used in sandy or muddy conditions. Avoid treading on zips (especially when wearing boots).

Once your tent is set up, if you notice wrinkles running from one corner to the next (on the interior floor), this means that you've pulled the tent too tightly in that direction. Reposition the pegs until the floor evens out.

Tents made of synthetic material will expand or contract with temperature changes and should be re-tensioned to ensure proper performance.

If your tent does not have a sewn in groundsheet, in bad weather, raise the edges of the groundsheet with wood. This forces the rainwater underneath the groundsheet.

Tent care

Ground Cloth/Carpet inside your tent

You can use an old rug or even an old blanket to provide a comfy and warm base to your tent. Some models of tents even have carpets that are made specifically for them. (You do have to pay extra!). It will protect your tent bottom from protruding objects.

Sunshine

Don't leave your tent in the sun for prolonged periods. Ultraviolet rays damage the tent fabric and its waterproofing capabilities. If you can, set up in the shade.

Tent Tips

Unless it's raining open up your tent every day. If it's dry roll up the sides but if wet hang them up to dry/air. During the night you will breath out carbon dioxide and water vapour and airborne germs. Opening up the tent makes sure that this is blown out and will make your tent a far more pleasant place to be. Baking soda is useful for deodorizing tents and sleeping bags, removing stains and also as a cleanser. Put an old rug or a piece of outdoor carpet in front of your tent to reduce the amount of dirt tracked in.

Sweep out your tent

Always keep the inside of your tent free from dirt. Accumulated dirt between your sleeping bag and the floor will gradually erode the tent floor.

Kids and Camping

A great way to prepare kids for camping is setting up the tent in the back garden. They will love it and it will help them to learn to put the tent up and take it down.

If you have a young family it is best to have one family tent. If you have older children you could get them their own tent – it may be more fun for them and you can put them to bed and not have to disturb them when you go to bed.

Kids and wet weather

If you have a gazebo and picnic rug this will provide a dry area for the kids to play. Be prepared for rain – the general mood can quickly change if the weather changes, a gazebo will also prevent your tent from becoming all wet and muddy. Remember to take plenty of games, books and drawing supplies to keep them occupied.

If you are going on a longer holiday, it is a good idea to plan a few days' activities in advance. You can visit local attractions or go for a walk in the country. The campsite will provide you with a list of local sights and activities.

Waterproofs

It would be a good idea to invest in some waterproofs for the kids. This will help to keep their clothes drier and less muddy.

Sleeping equipment

You need to choose a suitable bed for them to sleep on and a nice warm sleeping bag, as this can be the key to a peaceful nights sleep for both them and you. Sleeping bags come in children's sizes and it is better to get a children's bag as they are smaller so there is less area for heat to escape.

Equipment

A head torch is a good idea for the kids and it is fun for them to wear too. If there are children around it is safer to use battery operated lighting as opposed to gas powered.

Chores

Kids will enjoy having jobs to do – collecting wood for the fire, fetching the water, and helping with the meals. Give each child a job to do each day, this will make them feel part of the whole camping experience.

Games and things to do

Children (and some adults) love to play games. You can take board games with you, although this can lead to pieces being lost of damaged by the elements, but you can also play others that are more spontaneous.

Chicken
Play catch with a water balloon – this is a good game for balmy summer nights.

Red Light/Green Light
In this game, one person plays the red light and the rest try to touch him/her. At the start, all the children form a line about 15 feet away from the red light. The red light faces away from the line of kids and says "green light". At this point the kids are allowed to move towards the red light. At any point, the red light may say "red light!" and turn around. If any of the kids are caught moving after this has occurred, they are out. Play resumes when the red light turns back around and says "green light". The red light wins if all the kids are out before anyone is able to touch him/her. Otherwise, the first player to touch the red light wins the game and earns the right to be red light for the next game.

Paper Race
For this game you will need 2 sheets of newspaper per person. You use the sheets as stepping stones. You can only stand on your two sheets and only one foot per sheet. Place one piece on the floor and put one foot on it, then place the other piece in front of it and put your other foot. Once the second foot is down the first foot can be lifted and the first sheet can be placed in front of the second sheet. This is repeated until you get to a given line and then back to the start. Players are only allowed to step on their own newspaper.

Frogger
First you need to pick a detective whose task it will be to try and find the frogger. Once the detective has been picked he or she needs to move away from the game area and cover their eyes so they can't see what will happen next. Then sit everyone in a circle and make them close their eyes - no peeking! Tell them that you are going to tap one person on the head and that this person will be the frogger. The frogger's role is to stick their tongue out at the other players in the circle without the detective seeing them. If the frogger sticks his or her tongue out at you then you are "frozen" at which point you should wait about 10 seconds and then

make a funny face and hold it. The detective now gets to guess the frogger, but if they are wrong the game continues with the frogger "freezing" more players until the frogger is discovered or all the players are "frozen"! Take it in turns to play frogger and detective.

Sardines
Someone is chosen as the sardine. That person then has to go and hide while everyone else closes their eyes and counts to 100. Then everyone has to look for the sardine. If a person finds the sardine they have to hide with the sardine and they become a sardine. The loser is the last one to find the sardines.

Here are a couple of games for the big kids!!

Who am I?
Everyone has a piece of paper and writes down a name of a famous person, either dead or alive. Then they stick the paper to the forehead of the person next to them. Post-it notes are great for this but normal paper is fine, all you need to do is lick it, or if the person is a bit funny about it, let them lick it! You must then take it in turns to ask questions about the person you are. You can only ask one question at a time and the other players can only answer yes or no. Play continues until everyone has guessed who they are.

Famous name game
Someone starts with the name of a famous person. The next player then has to think of a famous person with a first name beginning with the first letter of the last name. i.e. First person says 'Julie Garland' the next person has to say a name beginning with 'G' i.e. Gary Barlow, then the next person has to say a 'B' and it carries on. If someone says a name with the same letter for first and last name the direction of play reverses. Names cannot be repeated, the penalty for this is to do a forfeit or you are out of the game. You need to decide this before you start the game. This game can go on for as long as you like and the winner is the person with the least forfeits.

Never store your tent away when it's wet or damp. Consequences of forgetting this cardinal rule is mildew damage and a smelly tent. So, before you pack it away ensure it is totally dry. Either lay it out in a shady spot (do not leave in direct sunlight) or take it home and then dry it on the washing line or in the garage/house. It won't take long to dry out and then you can put it away in its storage bag.

Sometimes condensation may be an issue, especially in certain types of tents. One of the ways to combat this is to spray the outside of your tent with a waterproofing spray which beads up water so it rolls off the tent's surface (think of water rolling off a duck's back). You can buy this from any camping retailer; you will need to ask to find out which brand would suit your tent.

Packaging of your tent
Constantly folding your tent the same way will eventually cause creases that will compromise its weatherproofing and ultimately crack the fabric itself. So bear that in mind and try to fold it in different ways.

To dismantle your tent, follow the specific erection instructions in reverse order.

Removing Pegs
Use a peg extractor or another peg to pull them out. Never use the rubber ring, tensioners or the fabric of the tent.

Removing Poles
Dismantle poles carefully. Flexible shock-corded poles should be pushed out through the sleeves not pulled.

Packing
Clean off any mud or grass and fold the tent with the zips partly open and then roll up towards the doors so that the air can escape. Ideally the zips should then be fully closed.

Poles and pegs should be packed separately from the tent to avoid damage.

Before storing your tent for any period, make sure that it is completely dry and all mud has been removed. Tents are best stored opened out in a dry, well-aired place. If this is not possible, give the tent a really good airing on a dry day or indoors if necessary.

Ensure that the zip webs and all tapes are dry before storing back in its bag. Store the pegs and the poles separately in bag provided.

When you get home
As you put everything away, make a note of what you didn't use, so that you don't bother taking it in future.

Make a shopping list for anything you wished you had brought with you and either add this to your storage tub or put it on your permanent checklist. It's also a good idea to make your own personal packing list so you can simply grab what you need next time without having to spend time thinking about it.

And finally....book your next trip.

Checklists for your trip

Shelter
Tent
Mallet
Gazebo
Windbreaks

Camp furniture
Camp chairs
Table
Camp kitchen
Picnic mat

Clothes
Day clothes
Nightclothes
Shoes
Boots
Swimming costumes
Coats and hats
Waterproofs

Sleeping
Airbeds/camp bed/mat
Sleeping bags
Pillows
Extra blankets/throws

Lighting
Gas/Battery powered lamps
Spare batteries
Matches and/or gas lighter
Citronella candles

Entertainment
Musical instruments
Paper, pens, etc.
Books and toys
Football

Eating and drinking
Water carrier, tap and stand
Water purification tablets
Stove
Fridge (ensure you leave enough time to pre-chill it before adding food) and/or cool box
Gas, regulator and hose for each appliance (check the gas levels in each tank)
Cutlery
Plates, cups, bowls, beakers (crockery and paper)
Cooking utensils
Chopping mats
Measuring jug
Mixing bowl
Saucepans
Frying pan
Kettle
Paper towels
Folding crates for carrying/storing food
Washing-up bowl, liquid, cloths and brush
2 x tea towels

Personal care

UV protection and sunglasses
Moisturising cream
Facial cleansing lotion
Cotton wool balls
First aid kit
Medication for the duration of the camp, if appropriate
Hairbrushes
Deodorant
Towels
Toothbrushes
Toothpaste
Sanitary protection
Toilet rolls
Make-up
Wet wipes
Soap
Shampoo and conditioner
Shower gel

Small children's things

Pushchair/buggy (with rain cover, parasol)
Wipes
Nappies
Potty

Miscellaneous

Directions to the site, tickets, maps and other paperwork
Mobile phone and recharging cable
Money
Swiss Army knife
Compass and Map
Safety pins
Camera (remember to charge before you go)
Camcorder
Clothesline and pegs
Basic tools (screwdrivers, pliers, etc.)

Pets

Bedding
Food and bowls
Leads (you are not allowed to let your dog off the lead at most campsites)

The hints, tips and recipes contained in this book are passed on in good faith but the publisher cannot be held responsible for any adverse results. Please be aware that certain recipes may contain nuts. Spoon measurements are level, teaspoons are assumed to be 5ml, tablespoons 15ml. For other measurements, see chart below. Times given are for guidance only, as preparation techniques may vary and can lead to different cooking times.

Spoons to millilitres

1/2 teaspoon	2.5 ml	1 Tablespoon	15 ml
1 teaspoon	5 ml	2 Tablespoons	30 ml
1-1 1/2 teaspoons	7.5 ml	3 Tablespoons	45 ml
2 teaspoons	10 ml	4 Tablespoons	60 ml

Grams to ounces

10g	0.25oz	225g	8oz
15g	0.38oz	250g	9oz
25g	1oz	275g	10oz
50g	2oz	300g	11oz
75g	3oz	350g	12oz
110g	4oz	375g	13oz
150g	5oz	400g	14oz
175g	6oz	425g	15oz
200g	7oz	450g	16oz

Metric to cups

Description		
Flour etc	115g	1 cup
Clear honey etc	350g	1 cup
Liquids etc	225ml	1 cup

Liquid measures

5fl oz	1/4 pint	150 ml
7.5fl oz		215 ml
10fl oz	1/2 pint	275 ml
15fl oz		425 ml
20fl oz	1 pint	570 ml
35fl oz		1 litre

This edition first published in 2009 by ImPulse Paperbacks, an imprint of Iron Press Ltd. © Iron Press Ltd 2009 Printed in China